ISBN 978-0-484-43118-7
PIBN 10609072

This book is a reproduction of an important historical work. Forgotten Books uses
state-of-the-art technology to digitally reconstruct the work, preserving the original format
whilst repairing imperfections present in the aged copy. In rare cases, an imperfection in
the original, such as a blemish or missing page, may be replicated in our edition. We do,
however, repair the vast majority of imperfections successfully; any imperfections that
remain are intentionally left to preserve the state of such historical works.

SOCIETY

OF THE

FIFTY-FIRST REGIMENT

PENNSYLVANIA VETERAN VOLUNTEERS.

RECORD OF PROCEEDINGS

OF THE

FIRST ANNUAL REUNION,

HELD AT

NORRISTOWN, PA., Sept. 17, 1880.

HARRISBURG, PA.:

LANE S. HART, PRINTER.

1880.

SOCIETY

OF THE

FIFTY-FIRST REGIMENT PENN'A VETERAN VOLUNTEERS,

The surviving members of the Fifty-first Regiment Pennsylvania Veteran Volunteers, held their first annual reunion at Norristown, September 17, 1880.

The Veterans assembled at Zook Post Room, at nine o'clock, and after the Norristown Cornet Band had played a dirge in front of the monument in the public square, a procession was formed on Main street, right resting on Swede, and under the command of General William J. Bolton, proceeded to Globe Park.

The members of the regiment wore red badges, on which was inscribed "Society Fifty-first Regiment Pennsylvania Veteran Volunteers, Ninth Army Corps." The guests wore blue badges. Many houses were decorated in honor of the occasion. Six of the old battle-flags of the regiment were carried in the procession, Company "F," Sixth Regiment National Guard, acting as escort.

The procession moved to the Park by the way of Swede and Marshall streets. At the Park, the dining-room of the hotel was handsomely decorated with a large number of American flags, and nine tables had been spread, capable of seating three hundred guests.

ment, and the companies from other parts of the State were thrown into the left wing. By request of your President, I bid the left wing a hearty welcome here to-day. It was remarkable how the regiment became unified, without reference to locality.

Continuing, the speaker gave a number of reminiscences of the war, and the battle of Antietam. In conclusion, he said:

"Now the right wing of this regiment, from this county, greets the left wing from different parts of the State. [Applause.] It also greets our comrades who have served in other commands, and one that was as much perhaps, or nearly so, and perhaps more a Montgomery county regiment than even the Fifty-first. I refer to the gallant One Hundred and Thirty-eighth. We welcome them. We welcome all. We welcome the citizens. We are glad to see you all, and hope that we may be able to meet in the future from year to year, and see your faces as we see them to day, pleasant and smiling."

Three cheers were given for General Hartranft.

The Secretary read the minutes of the previous meetings:

NORRISTOWN, *March* 21, 1880.

In pursuance to a notice, a meeting was held by the members of the late Fifty-first Regiment Pennsylvania Veteran Volunteers, to take steps for forming a regimental association.

General William J. Bolton was called to the chair, and Edward Schall was chosen Secretary.

On motion of Comrade Schall, the chairman was instructed to procure copies of the constitution and by-laws of similar organizations, and submit them to a future meeting.

General Bolton stated that General Hartranft had in his possession two or three hundred copies of the "History of the Fifty-first," and had agreed to give one copy to each member joining the association, and paying whatever initiation fee might be decided upon.

The chairman was instructed to appoint a committee to ascertain, so far as possible, the address of all surviving members of the regiment, and notify them of the action taken. Also, to set the time and place for another meeting.

On motion adjourned, to meet at the call of the chairman.

WILLIAM J. BOLTON,
President.

EDWARD SCHALL,
Secretary.

NORRISTOWN, *May 25*, 1880.

The meeting was called to order by the chairman, who announced that the object of the meeting was to adopt a constitution and by-laws for the government of the organization.

Comrades Edward Schall, William W. Owens, and John Gilligan, of the Committee on Constitution and By-Laws, submitted the following :

CONSTITUTION.

ARTICLE I.

Tiis association shall be known as the "Society of the Fifty-first Regiment Pennsylvania Veteran Volunteers."

ARTICLE II.

Every member of the Fifty-first Regiment Pennsylvania Veteran Volunteers, who was honorably discharged, or who remains in the regular service of the United States, shall be entitled to membership in this society, upon subscribing to its constitution and by-laws, and paying the fee therein specified.

ARTICLE III.

The object of the society is to perpetuate the history of the above command to which its members were attached; and whilst cherishing the honored memory of those of their comrades who fell in the cause of their country, it shall be its endeavor, by an annual reunion, to promote and preserve among the survivors the feeling of friendship and good-fellowship for which they have hitherto been distinguished.

ARTICLE IV.

The officers of this society shall consist of a President, Vice President, Secretary, and Treasurer, who shall be elected annually, at the regular meeting. A majority of the members present shall have the power to elect their officers. The President, at each annual meeting, shall appoint an Executive Committee, consisting of one from each company and one at large, for the ensuing year, whose duty it shall be to make the proper arrangement for the next meeting of the society.

ARTICLE V.

The regular meetings shall take place not oftener than once a year, and at such time and place as may be determined by a majority of the members, at the regular meeting next preceding.

Members will be expected to attend the regular meetings, or if unable to do so, will give the Secretary timely notice, in writing, of their inability, and its cause.

ARTICLE VI.

Any member who shall be in arrears for dues for a period of three years shall have his name dropped from the rolls until his dues shall be paid, or they be remitted by a vote of the society.

ARTICLE VII.

Honoring the achievements of their brothers-in-arms, this society authorizes the President or Executive Committee to invite to its meetings any persons who have served with distinction in the army or navy of the United States.

BY-LAWS.

ARTICLE I.

An initiation fee of twenty-five cents, and an annual fee of twenty-five cents, shall be paid by each member to the Secretary, and by him to the Treasurer.

ARTICLE II.

Money, for the necessary expenses of the society, may be expended by the Treasurer, upon the approval of the President.

ARTICLE III.

The Treasurer shall make a report to the annual meeting of all receipts and expenditures, with vouchers.

ARTICLE IV.

The Secretary shall report to every meeting all correspondence of general interest.

ARTICLE V.

All questions and resolutions shall be decided by a majority of the members present. But amendments to the Constitution shall require the assent of two thirds of the members present at a regular meeting.

ARTICLE VI.

In the meeting of this society, the members thereof shall be designated as Comrades.

ARTICLE VII.

The order of business shall be as follows :

1. Reading the journal of the previous meeting.

2. Appointment of committees on business, and for nomination of officers.

3. Receiving reports.

4. Current business.

5. Election of officers.

6. Adjournment.

An election of officers, to serve until the next annual meeting, was then held, with the following result:

*President—*WILLIAM J. BOLTON.

*Vice President—*M. L. SCHOCK.

*Secretary—*EDWARD SCHALL.

*Treasurer—*WILLIAM W. OWENS.

The meeting adjourned, to meet at the call of the President.

WILLIAM J. BOLTON,

EDWARD SCHALL,   *President.*

Secretary.

———

NORRISTOWN, *August* 10, 1880.

Met at the office of Comrade Schall, General Bolton in the chair.

The following Executive Committee was appointed, to wit: Adjutant Jacob H. Santo, Captain J. Merrill Linn, Captain John A. Gillilland, Captain Henry Jacobs, Lieutenant John Genther, Lieutenant John Gilligan, Lieutenant Lewis Patterson, Sergeant Isaac E. Fillman,

Sergeant John C Dittler, Corporal Samuel Egolf, and Private Joseph A. Logan.

On motion, it was decided to hold the first annual reunion in Norristown, on Friday, September 17, 1880, the eighteenth anniversary of the battle of Antietam.

The chairman announced that Captain J. Merrill Linn would deliver an oration, and Honorable George N. Corson a poem, at the reunion on the 17th instant.

WILLIAM J. BOLTON,

EDWARD SCHALL, *President.*

Secretary.

———

NORRISTOWN, *August* 24, 1880.

Met at Comrade Schall's office, in the court-house.

The President appointed the following committee to make the necessary arrangements for the reunion of the regiment: Sergeant Isaac E. Fillman, Corporal Daniel Lare, Lieutenant John Gilligan, Corporal Andrew Fair, Captain Henry Jacobs, Samuel Daub, Samuel McCarter, Samuel Taylor, Lieutenant Lewis Patterson, and Amandus Gargus. They are also authorized to collect funds.

On motion, the Norristown Cornet Band was engaged to play at the reunion.

On motion, the services of Company " F," Sixth Regiment Pennsylvania National Guard, for escort duty at the reunion, were accepted.

On motion adjourned.

WILLIAM J. BOLTON,

EDWARD SCHALL, *President.*

Secretary.

The following committee was appointed on nomination of officers: William H. Yerkes, Theodore Gilbert, William W. Owens, M. L. Schock, and John Genther. They reported:

President—WILLIAM J. BOLTON.

Vice President—M. L. SCHOCK.

Secretary—EDWARD SCHALL.

Treasurer—W. W. OWENS.

Their report was unanimously approved.

It was decided to hold the next annual reunion at Lewisburg, Pa., on September 14, 1881, the anniversary of the battle of South Mountain.

The Secretary read the following letters:

COMMONWEALTH OF PENNSYLVANIA,

EXECUTIVE CHAMBER,

HARRISBURG, *September* 13, 1880.

General WILLIAM J. BOLTON,

Norristown, Pa:

DEAR SIR: I am directed by the Governor to inform you that his engagements are such as to prevent his acceptance of your kind invitation to attend the first reunion of the Fifty-first Regiment Pennsylvania Veteran Volunteers, to be held at Globe Park, Norristown, on Friday, September 17, 1880.

Very truly yours,

WARREN B. KEELY,

Executive Clerk.

BELLEFONTE, *Sepetmber* 13, 1880.

GENTLEMEN: Please accept my thanks .for your invitation to the reunion of the Fifty-first Regiment Pennsylvania Veteran Volunteers, on the 17th of September.

Rest assured it would give me much pleasure to meet the survivors of that gallant regiment, but it is quite impossible for me to leave my home this week.

With my best wishes for a good time to all present,

I remain truly your friend,

A. G. CURTIN.

Major General HARTRANFT, Major General BOLTON, and others.

———

MENTOR, OHIO, *September* 11, 1880.

General W. BOLTON,

Norristown, Pa.:

DEAR SIR: I have received yours of the 9th instant, inviting me to attend your reunion on the 17th instant, but my engagements render it impossible for me to be with you at that time. -Regretting this,

I am very truly yours,

J. A. GARFIELD.

———

GOVERNOR'S ISLAND, NEW YORK HARBOR,

August 31, 1880.

DEAR SIRS: I am in receipt of your invitation of the 2d instant, and, while thanking you for the courtesy extended to me, regret that I shall be unable to leave my post of duty at the time indicated for the reunion. With best wishes, I am very truly yours,

WINFIELD S. HANCOCK.

General J. F. HARTRANFT, General W. J. BOLTON, and others.

EDGEHILL, BRISTOL, R. I., *September* 4, 1880.

MY DEAR GENERAL: I have delayed answering your kind invitation to meet my old comrades of the gallant Fifty-first on the 17th instant, in the hope that I might accept it, but much to my sorrow, I find it impossible to do so. Please present me, in great friendship, to our comrades and your good wife, and believe me,

Faithfully your friend,

A. E. BURNSIDE.

———

CINCINNATI, *September* 14, 1880.

General WILLIAM J. BOLTON,

Norristown, Pa. :

DEAR SIR : Your favor of the 30th of July, inviting me to attend the reunion of the Fifty-first Regiment Pennsylvania Veteran Volunteers, at Norristown, on the 17th instant, received, and I very much regret that important business appointments in Michigan will prevent my being present on that important and interesting occasion. It would afford me much pleasure to meet my old friends and comrades, and assist them in establishing a society for the perpetuation of the history of the Fifty-first regiment, and at the same time to promote and strengthen the bonds of friendship and brotherhood among the members living. And, while speaking of ourselves, don't let us forget those of our members who died that the NATION might live. And let us renew our pledge that the principles for which they fought and died must and shall prevail. Wishing you all a pleasant and happy re-union, I remain

Yours, very truly,

J. W. IREDELL, Jr.

Enclosed find an application for membership and fee, twenty-five cents.

———

PHILADELPHIA, *September* 16, 1880.

Generals JOHN F. HARTRANFT, WILLIAM J. BOLTON, *and others, Committee :*

GENTLEMEN : I have the honor to acknowledge the re-ceipt of your polite invitation to participate in the re-union of the Fifty-first Regiment Pennsylvania Veteran Volunteers, and banquet attending the same, and I thank you most heartily.

I always remember the old Fifty-first with feelings of warm comradeship. I can never forget how, at Antietam, when relieved by the Forty-eighth, on the crest overlook-ing Sharpsburg, the Fifty-first, although without a cart-ridge, bravely remained supporting the Forty-eighth, determined not to give up the hill without a trial of cold steel before yielding.

I expected to be there, promising myself much pleas-ure, but I find now I cannot be present. Regretting this, and wishing you a delightful time, I am, truly and fraternally,

Yours,

O. C. BOSBYSHELL.

FERNANDINA, FLA., *September* 3, 1880.

DEAR GENERAL: I received your invitation to attend a reunion of the Fifty-first Regiment Pennsylvania Veteran Volunteers, at Norristown, Pa., on the 17th instant, and should have been much pleased to meet my old comrades on such an occasion. But previous to receiving your invitation, I had arranged to be present at the annual meeting of the "Society of the Army of the Cumberland," at Toledo, Ohio, September 22. I enclose my application for membership, and hope every honorably discharged member of the old regiment will become a member of the society. Although not able to be with you in person on the 17th instant, I will be in spirit, and will recall to mind the noble old regiment as I saw it on the same date eighteen years before, as it charged and carried the Burnside bridge at Antietam, in its usual gallant style, but at such fearful cost of life and limb. Hoping to attend some future meetings, and with kindest regards to all, I remain,

Very truly yours,

J. C. READ.

To General WILLIAM J. BOLTON, *President Fifty-first Regiment Pennsylvania Veteran Volunteers, Norristown, Pa.*

———

GRAND RAPIDS, MICH., *September* 10, 1880.

WILLIAM J. BOLTON, *President Society Fifty-first Penn. Veteran Volunteers, Norristown, Pa.* :

DEAR SIR : Your invitation to attend a reunion of the above society on the 17th of this month, is received. 'I greatly regret that business engagements will prevent my attendance; but while I cannot be with you personally on that day, I cannot forget your meeting, nor the day that celebrated the anniversary of one of the hardest fought battles of the late war, eighteen years ago, in which the old Fifty-first struck a blow that decided the day.

Extend the hand of good fellowship to any of my old comrades who may be with you on the occasion of your meeting, and whilst recounting scenes of hard campaigns, tread lightly and shed silent tears over the graves of fallen comrades, who died to preserve a nation of which we are so proud to-day.

I trust that these reunions may continue from year to year, until the last member of the society will have ans-wered to the final roll-call—Death.

With my best wishes for the success of the meeting, believe me to be,

Very truly yours,

HENRY B. WETZELL.

———

WASHINGTON, *September* 13, 1880.

General WILLIAM J. BOLTON, *President Society of the Fifty-first Regiment Pennsylvania Veteran Volunteers:*

DEAR GENERAL: Very much to my regret, I find it im-possible to be present at the reunion of the Fifty-first regiment on the 17th instant. If not asking too much ·for one who added so little to the honor and fame of the regiment, I would thank you to convey my hearty good

wishes to all comrades who may kindly bear me in remembrance.

During the brief period of life remaining to us, it is
certainly very proper that the survivors of the Fifty-first
regiment should muster annually to revive cherished
memories, and to strengthen friendships which can never
die. We should muster under the old flag, dear to every
loyal heart, to renew the vows of perpetual allegiance to
our common country.

The day you have selected for the first annual meeting,
the anniversary of the battle of Antietam, could not be
more opportune. On that day we again hear, above the
wild crash, with the same thrilling sensations, the voice
of the aid-de-camp saying to the brave Sturgis: "General Burnside calls upon Colonel Hartranft and the Fifty-
first Pennsylvania to take the stone bridge at all hazards."
On that day we can renew affectionate memories for the
honored dead, and on that day we can renew our warm
sympathy for all those who walk cheerfully through life,
maimed and disabled, that the nation might live.

Anticipating for you a successful and happy reunion, I
remain,

Very truly, your comrade,

H. C. Wood.

New York, *September* 13, 1880.

My Dear General: Your kind letter of the 2d instant has just reached me. I thank you and the members
of the Fifty-first Regiment Pennsylvania Volunteers for
their kind remembrance. I regret exceedingly that busi-

ness engagements of great importance preclude the pos-
sibility of my accepting their kind invitation for the 17th
instant. Say to them, dear general, that the many ex-
ploits of bravery performed by the old regiment are always first in my memory.

Yours, respectfully,

E. W. FERRERO.

General J. F. HARTRANFT.

FLUSHING, L. I., *September* 11, 1880.

My Brothers in Arms :

DEAR COMRADES: I acknowledge the receipt of your
kind invitation to be with you on the 17th, and also the
postal wishing me to become a member of your society,
which I will do heartily, but sorry I can't be with you at
your reunion.

I never will forget the Fifty-first above all other regiments that were offered to support the battery, and by
your invitation I see you have not forgotten the Thirty-
fourth.

The Fifty-first and Thirty-fourth, together with the
Ninth Corps, stood a unit through shot and shell, from
the Wilderness to the taking of Petersburg. At Antietam,
especially, I remember the bravery of the Fifty-first.
The charge that was made by the Ninth Corps at the
stone bridge was grand, equal to the famous charge of
Napoleon at the Bridge of Lodi. Such bravery as our
boys exhibited is rarely known.

JACOB RUMER,

Late Captain 34th Battery, and Brevet Major U.S.V.

The present Executive Committee was continued. Its members are: Adjutant Jacob H. Santo, Captain J. Merrill Linn, Captain John R. Gillilland, Captain Henry Jacobs, Lieutenant John H. Gentier, Lieutenant Join Gilligan, Lieutenant Lewis Patterson, Sergeant Isaac E. Fillman, Sergeant John C. Dettler, Corporal Samuel Egolf, and Private Joseph A. Logan.

On motion, the Vice President, M. L. Sciock, was requested to appoint an auxilliary committee from members of the regiment residing in and near Lewisburg.

He announced the following committee: M. G. Reed, John V. Rule, B. B. Harris, Albert List, J. P. Brooke, D. H. Getz, Ciarles Schnure, William F. Campbell, and David Brewer.

On motion of General Hartranft, tie proceedings of the annual meeting, with the names and residences of the members present, were ordered to be printed in pamphlet form.

Tie following closing prayer was offered by tie Reverend H. M. Kieffer, pastor of the "Ciurch of the Ascension," Norristown, Pennsylvania:

Almighty God, Our Heavenly Father, we give Tiee most hearty thanks and praise for the goodness and mercy we have enjoyed at Thy hand tiis day. We acknowledge with gratitude our dependence upon Tiee, and tiank Thee that Thou hast preserved our lives, and permitted us to meet here this day in iealth and strengti, to revive old memories and to renew the friendsiips formed in tie dark and terrible days of tie past. To Tiy mercy it is we owe our lives: for it was by Thy strong iand tiat all of us were delivered, in the years gone by, from the terror by night and from the arrow that flyeth by day. It was of Thy mercy that neither the pestilence that walketh in darkness, nor the destruction that wasteth at noonday, came nigh unto us : and that while a thousand fell at our side and ten thousand at our right hand, yet have we been permitted to live long in the land the Lord, our God, hath given us.   We thank Thee for the kind Providence which has been over us during the years that have elapsed since those dark days of the war ; and we pray Thee that, as Thou hast been with us in the past, both in war and in peace, so also Thou wilt be gracious unto us in all future time.   Crown with Thy favor and blessing, we beseech Thee, the exercises of this day : watch over us throughout life, and when life's warfare is ended, and its fitful fever past, grant unto us all that great peace which passeth all understanding, through Jesus Christ, our Lord and Redeemer, Amen.

At one o'clock the comrades re-assembled for dinner, at the hotel. After dinner, Captain J. Merrill Linn delivered the following oration:

CAPTAIN LINN'S ORATION.

An eventful life often comes from seeming chance. In looking back over it, we can see the turn where, by a handsbreadth, it might have gone with us a thousand other ways—it is idle to speculate how—it is enough if only, in after years, we can recall it with pride and with pleasure.

One day in November, 1861, Colonel Hartranft and Lieutenant Colonel Bell—peace be to his ashes! whose gifted soul on this day, eighteen years ago, sped on its flight to its home beyond the blue light,

> " And we know
> A solemn joy, that one whose manhood glow
> Faded so soon, should die to mark how grand,
> Above all fleeting life, to die for Native land."

Our colonel and lieutenant colonel went into Govcruor Curtiu's room at the capitol, and announced that the regiment was full, and they were ready to march.

The Governor said there was an expedition fitting out, called the Coast Division, and he would telegraph to Thomas A. Scott, then Assistant Secretary of War, for a place in it.

An order came, and on the night of the 18th of November, 1861, in the broad fall moonlight, beneath the wide-spreading ancient elms of St. John's College, at Annapolis, Maryland, we piled our arms.

A fateful move! Our life became one with that of an army corps, whose armed tread was heard upon the reedy shores of the old North State; whose bronzed faces and stalwart arms stayed an exultant foe from Cedar Mountain to the Potomac; whose sudden push won the stone bridge at Antietam; who spared not their blood on the slopes of Fredericksburg; who sustained the arm of their gallant commander when he issued the famous order No. 38; who shared in the capture of Vicksburg; who, in the morning light of that lovely July day, unfurled their flags and deployed their columns on the hills about Jackson; that from the bridge at Lenoir, by Cambell's station, to the fort crowned hills of Knoxville, baffled and held at bay the famous corps of Longstreet; that crossed the Rapidan on the 4th of May, 1864, and went by the way of the Wilderness Court House, and Cold Harbor, where fell our gallant Schall, across the James; that held so long the lines of Petersburg, where, in that last grand, final rush, when the Fifty-first, under Bolton, held the brigade line at Fort Steadman, and crowned the crest of the crater, where eighteen months before they suffered so much, and pierced the lines that so long held our armies at bay. That you were among this armed throng; that you bore yourselves up proudly to meet the coming fight; that you stood staunchly by when the death shot fell thick and fast, when the crashing shell broke through the serried column, and the sheeted lead withered the steady ranks; that through the midnight march, through the pelting rain and sleeting snow, you gathered your numbers with unfailing strength, and hearts that never quailed;

that you carried your colors to the end, and placed them
again in the hands that gave them to you, not, indeed,
with the fresh crimson flush and unstained azure hue of
their newly born beauty, but rent and torn from the
fields of many battles; may now well kindle the eye,
may well now mantle the cheek with blood from a quicker
heart's pulse at their remembrance.

But as the Fifty-first regiment of Pennsylvania rises
higher than its individual life in its place in the Ninth
Army Corps, and still higher in its place in the Grand
Army of the Republic, it is still higher and grander in its
place in the world's progress.

If there is one thing more clearly taught than another
in the history of mankind, in all its records, sacred and
profane, it is that every material step toward freedom,
freedom of the body, freedom of the mind, freedom of
the soul, is worked out in blood. The history of the
liberal party, in every progressive nation, is written in
blood. It is one of continued strife and struggle. It is
necessarily aggressive. Not that it is in its soul blood-
thirsty; not that it is in itself turbulent, or in its heart
discontented, but that this is the price that must be paid
for freedom to act in such a way as to have secure life,
liberty, and the pursuit of happiness.

Oppression and wrong are conservative. Old forms of
life, having served the purpose for which they were crea-
ted, are taken possession of by the tireless spirit of evil,
which never quits its watch upon the effort of the human
race to better itself. That which once helped, now be-
comes its bonds, and again and again it must rise in its

might and burst them asunder. Oppression and wrong
do not let go easily. If they must quit, they turn and
rend their victim, and leave him prostrate, though free,
like the demon of old.

Right is higher than life; therefore the soldier battles
for it. There is no prouder place among men, than that
of the citizen soldier.

It is for no idle romance that the heart beats with
quicker pulse at the roll of the drum; that the bugle-call
starts the blood in a swifter current; that the soul rises
when the ear catches the sound of the tread of armed
men. The dancing plume, the bayonet glittering in the
sunlight, the flash of the saber and the rattle of the car-
bine, the clash of the musket, the jingle of the spur, the
ring of the iron hoof on the stony road, the roar of the
artillery, the streaming guidon and waving flag, the gilded
trappings, all that pomp of the moving column have their
effect upon us, not because they are glitter and noise,
but because they are an appropriate expression of the
power of men; of men stirred to the inmost depths;
now ready to use both arm and brain, to do and dare,
with all the might that God has given to man, trained to
it with all the skill of man's device. Just as appropriate
as is of nature's power, when the leaves clap their hands
in gladsome dance in the morning air, in the sunlight;
as when the oak bends in the rising storm; as when the
lightnings flash, the thunder rolls, as the resounding surf
on the old ocean's shore.

But, as in the moving column of the army, its strength
is not in the individual effort, however bold and brave,

but in the concentration of individual effort. So what is effected by this concentration, is the true glory of the soldier.

The soldier leaves his home, all that he loves. There is no harder strain upon the heart, than when one in full life turns to part with that which is now his, which he might still keep if he wills it, but which he now, of set purpose, quits, with no assured hope that it will ever be his again.

He gives up that individual freedom, which has been a great part of his happiness, for the crowded barrack or camp. He puts himself under the stern command of another, endures the drill, that wearisome preparation for that which is still more weary, the march, the guard duty, the picket, which are all beset with disease, danger, and distress.

Then he comes to meet his foe, and with him he must engage in a death grapple.

That long stride for days and nights to reach the place, the sullen boom of the single gun in the early gray of the morning; the sharp crack of the rifle; the volley of musketry, and then the continuous roar, amid which comes the hurtling shell, as it falls with a crash into a rank, and the sharp sing of the ball that is dealing fast with all around; the sharp sting, the sickening thud, and the jarring crash.

The gathering of all the remaining energies to breast the stern onset, or for the rush to crown the crest of the death-dealing entrenchment!

The long nights and days of pain which no hand can

stay, but which must be endured until nature triumphs or succumbs! To fall helpless amid the burning forests; whose stealthy fires creep upon him, and suck out life with their hot breath; to be taken captive to those foul places where life drained out in loathesome horror; to meet and endure all these things voluntarily, is the glory of the soldier's manhood. But this is not the crowning glory of the soldiers of the Civil War; not the crowning glory of the men of the Fifty-first Regiment of Pennsylvania Volunteers.

It lay in the object for which all these things were done and suffered. It lay in that which was attained in the victory of the effort.

In the established personality and sovereignty of our government; in the preserved nationality of our people, bequeathed to us by our fathers; handed down to us by the heroes of the Revolution.

What you did and what you suffered was in the line of duty. Were the results to stay with the mere overcoming force with force, as was done on this day eighteen years ago, when the two great armies met, which is here and now commemorated, they would be bygone like the sulphurous clouds that rose from the guns on that fateful day; like the marks of the struggle smoothed out by the clothing verdure.

This day was followed by the proclamation of freedom to the slave, that wonderful anomaly in our national life, but not by that alone, though that were great enough to signalize it. Those unruly tongues that inveigh against the personality of our Government, those rude hands that were stretched forth to tear its sovereignty from its throne, those savage forces that were gathered to break up its nationality, were there and then stayed. Light broke for the oppressed by the way; but, more than all that, the current of the world's onward progress, pent and dammed awhile, flowed on in its beneficent way. This was the perfection of the work. This places in the unfading light of marvelous story, the deeds of the men of the Fifty-first regiment of Pennsylvania.

The hope of the world is in the ideal personality and sovereignty of government; in the ideal nationality of its peoples. Government is part of the economy of the world; its vocation, the welfare of the people; its idea, a government of the people, by the people, for the people; its means of attainment, ideal personality, ideal sovereignty, free communal life, and ideal nationality; a personality that is sacred; sovereignty that brooks no opposing will; free communal life that permits every one to dwell under his own vine and fig tree; nationality as wide as the breadth of the borders of the land. The antagonists of these are centralization, imperialism, and States rights, which is the disintegration of nationality.

Three thousand years before the birth of our Lord, the valleys of the Euphrates and the Tigris teemed with a population which, in wealth and civilization, has never been exceeded.

The whole of Asia Minor, from the Aegean Sea to Mount Ararat, was crowded with cities such as have never since been built, whose people enjoyed a free communal life, that gave the utmost development to human

wishes.   Babylon, Nineveh, Palmyra, Damascus, Tyre
and Sidon, Jerusalem, Thebes—they are the synonyms
in our minds of human greatness.

The desolation of these lands began when the Assyrian
came down from Nineveh to the Nile ; when his kingdom
reposed on the Persian Gulf, the Caspian Sea, and the
Mediterranean ; came again when the Persian laid his
chains in the waters of the Hellespond ; again, when the
Macedonian strode from the fastness of his mountains to
the furthest Indies.   Imperial Rome spread her sway over
them.   The Arabian swept by the Euphrates and the sea.
The Turanian, the Mongolian, the Turcoman, flooded
them.

On the southern shore of the Euxine, the port of
Bythnia, on the break-up of the Persian empire, fell to
Othman, the commander of a body of Turcomans, who
had entered the service of the Sultan of Iconium.   Pushing through the unguarded passes of Mount Olympus, he
attacked the Byzantine Empire, and he and his successors
inherited its imperialism.   Pushing across the Bosphorus,
their power was scarcely stayed at the walls of Vienna.
The Turcoman became master of Asia Minor, Syria,
Egypt, Arabia, in fine, that wonderful agglomeration of
nations known as Turkey in Europe and Turkey in Asia.
In all these long centuries of wars, imperialism has over-
come communal life, and tribute to the foreign potentate,
more than the mere desolation of wars, has taken away
the life-blood of the people.

Notwithstanding it has been said that war should be
no more, in the last half of the nineteenth century, since

the year 1850, there have been the greatest conflicts known in the history of the world. Civilized nations now stand armed cap-a-pie. Universal military servitude has been established, and the hand of God's guidance in the wars is shown that they have all been directed to the establishment of govermental sovereignty and the gathering of the peoples under one nationality. The war of the Crimea, and later, the tremendous struggle in the Balkans, when Russia's people gathered around their Emperor and carried him into the war more than half unwilling, were the outgrowth of Slavonic nationality, to free them from the yoke of the Turcomans and gather their race beneath the double-headed imperial eagle of Russia.

The Danish monarch had to give up his German-speaking people in Schleswig and Holstein.

Italy, divided and despoiled since the days of imperial Rome, held under the Spaniard, the Austrian, the Bourbon, breathed her first breath of nationality when Solferino reddened her glacial morain. Austria laid down the iron crown of Lombardy and retired behind the Quadrilateral when she was crushed at Sadowa. The dissolute Bourbon quitted his kingdom before the victorious legions of Garibaldi. The States of Italy, by their free suffrage, placed the crown of the kingdom of Italy upon the head of Victor Immanuel, the gallant. Rome became her capital and Italy became a nation; united and free, from the Alps to the Adriatic.

With the crush of the armies at Sadowa ended the German confederacy. The German armies crossed the Rhine, gained the hills of Gravelotte, seized the French armies at Sedan with their Emperor, besieged Metz, environed Paris, and the German people, now a nation, placed the crown of the empire of Germany upon the head of Kaiser William, their commander-in-chief, while yet he had his headquarters in Versailles. Paris surrendered. The German armies retired, carrying with them Alsace and Lorraine. France became a republic after a desperate struggle with the Commune.

Stay but yet for a breath of time, and the Turcoman will cross the Bosphorus to his Bothnia. Not a trace of his footsteps will remain on the sands of Arabia. A nation will be gathered by the banks of the Euphrates, and Ararat, from his antediluvian height, will look down upon the Armenian, great, wise, and wealthy Syria will establish her kingdom, Jerusalem rebuild her walls, Greece look out upon the Ægeau and the freed isles of the archipelago, and replant her colonies on the shores of Asia Minor.

Time will not go back on his dial.

At the close of the revolutionary war of our own country, crowned with the surrender of the British army at Yorktown, a proclamation issued disbanding the armies of the United States, after a struggle of eight long years; a struggle which has surrounded those who were engaged in it with a halo of glory, and set them up among the heroes of the world. Washington, in his farewell to the army, after "adverting to the enlarged prospects of happiness opened by the confirmation of national independence and sovereignty, exhorts them to maintain the strongest attachment to the Union. He bade farewell to his officers at Fraund's Tavern, passing through a single

corps of light infantry, stepping into a barge at White-
hall, turned to them, took off his hat and waved them a
silent adieu, and they watched him in silence until shut
out from view by a point of the Battery."

That was the end of the war of the revolution. Liberty was gained. It had yet to be maintained. The
struggle has gone on through three generations of men,
culminating in the great civil war of the United States.
Just that nationality, just that sovereignty upon which the
father of our country congratulated his soldiers when he
parted with them, just that union for which he bade them
maintain the strongest attachment, was the question of
the fearful contest eighty years afterwards. Mark the
response of his people. At the close of this war, through
the streets of the city that bears his beloved name, down
the avenue that bears the name of our beloved State, past
the chieftain who had led them to victory, not a single
corps of light infantry, but two hundred thousand war-
seamed veterans marched, bearing the tattered flags of
an hundred battles.

It is an old and trite saying that "eternal vigilance is
the price of liberty." It is a common mistake, because
we forget that life is an ever onward-moving thing, that,
after gaining a material step, we think to rest at that,
while, in fact, the end of every effort is the beginning of
a new one. The result of every struggle is but a preparation for a new one. The enemies of liberty are never
eradicated. Like sin, they are always lying at the door.
They crowd the pathway of every nation from its birth,
ready to sting its feet on its chosen way, to tempt it into

by-paths, to beguile it into slumber, to fasten on it in unwary moments, and to crush it into helplessness.

Only entire wakefulness, only unceasing watchfulness, energies never relaxed, vigor unabated, will serve to keep the nation safe.

> "Thou, too, sail on, O Ship of State!.
> Sail on, O Union, strong and great!
> Humanity, with all its fears,
> With all its hopes of future years,
> Is hanging breathless on thy fate.
> We know what master laid thy keel!
> What workman wrought thy ribs of steel,
> Who made each mast, and sail, and rope,
> What anvils rang, what hammers beat,
> In what a forge and what a heat
> Were shaped the anchors of thy hope.
> Fear not each sudden sound and shock.
> 'Tis of the wave, and not the rock.
> 'Tis but the flapping of the sail,
> And not a rent made by the gale.
> In spite of rock and tempest's roar,
> In spite of false lights on the shore,
> Sail on, nor fear to breast the sea!
> Our hearts, our hopes are all with thee.
> Our hearts, our hopes, our prayers, our tears,
> Our faith, triumphant o'er our fears,
> Are all with thee; are all with thee!"

After music by the band, George N. Corson, Esquire, was presented, and read the following:

HEROIC POEM.

One April morn, in the year of our Lord
    One thousand eight hundred and sixty-one,
Americans read at their breakfast board
    The stirring words of Abraham Lincoln:
"I call for seventy-five thousand men
    To enforce the laws and save the nation!"
And quick the people answered, there and then,
    We come for our nation's pledged salvation.

Another morn, the clouds were darkening
    More and more, and the light of Freedom's sky
Was dim, as millions now stood hearkening
    To old Father Abraham's thunder cry:
"To arms! ye loyal sons of West and North,
    Our brothers of the South are mad for war:
Americans, from all the land come forth;
    Come, ye freeman, five hundred thousand more."

Then there beat the war-drum in every street,
    And rang the war-cry in every household.
Back went the answer with liberty sweet
    To the bondsmen in treason's stronghold,
And joyous to the President's mighty heart:
    "We are coming, Father Abraham, aye,
Five hundred thousand more; and we will start
    Freedom's battle-cry for every slave to-day."

As State after State of the South went out,
  So State after State of the North proved true.
Companies moved, regiments formed, as the wild shout
  Rang out for Union and Liberty too.
The Fifty-first Regiment bounded forth
  In this darkest hour of the nation's day,
To fight this twin cause by the side of the North.
  And to hurl the rebel pretenders away.

It was in the autumn of sixty-one;
  Camp Curtin, Harrisburg, was drowned in rain,
When the grand forward movement was begun,
  And thoughts of war were a relief from pain.
For constraint to noble souls is a hell—
  They are forever restless for the right;
The soldier seeks the sound of shot and shell,
  And longs to lead his comrades in the fight.

They formed a camp at old Annapolis,
  Upon the banks of Susquehanna's tide,
And all honor to them whose fame with his
  Was to grow with time, they call it BURNSIDE.
Hartranft, Bell, and Schall, uniformed and snug
  With their ten Captains, to their tents invite us,
Bolton, Bell, Allebaugh, Schall, Hassenplug,
  Taylor, Snyder, Linn, Pechin, and Titus.

These were the school-boy days of the great school
  Of the war, when, to while away the time
Between the hours of drill and rigorous rule,
  Games and jokes and songs made up a merry chime;

And not the least in those days of camp-life,
    To ease the irk of mind and head and hand,
Was the music that rose above all strife
    From the noble boys in George Arnold's band.

Amid the January rain and snow,
    In the eventful year of sixty-two,
The men marched from their camp, and glad to go
    On "Cossack and Scout." But where? no one knew!
But now the news ran up and down the ships,
    The boys all sang, glad with new ambition,
"We are," with "hips, hurrahs," "hurrahs and hips,"
    "We are of the Burnside Expedition."

Thence followed Roanoke Island and Newbern,
    Camden, and the death of Colonel Bell
At Antietam, where never to return,
    Thousands moved sternly forward and thousands fell.
Ay, here Hartranft, wounded Bolton, and the boys,
    Like Lane S. Hart, who felt the rebel shot,
Have made a name exceed the fame of Troy's,
    And Antietam Bridge a Monumental spot.

Hunsicker, Coulston, Beaver, Somerlot, Marks, Davis,
    Herd, McDade, McMullin, and Captain Bell,
Private Lonsdale—all who helped to save us,
    And at Antietam or Fredericksburg fell,
Are names near and dear to you and us to-day.
    And in many a household there live those
Around us who weep to think they must obey,
    The fate which gave these loved ones to our foes.

On the Rappahannock, at Sulphur Springs,
   At Falmouth, and on the pontoons that bore
To Fredericksburg—there like the ancient kings
   The Fifty-first stood foremost in the war.
Steadfast from the ocean shore, at the East,
   Westward to red Mississippi's waters.
On the weary march, at the frugal feast,
   Or amidst the hell and yell of slaughters.

He who visits the Wilderness in years
   To be will seek the place where poor Kevin
Fell bearing the colors aloft with cheers'
   For the good old flag—then flew to Heaven;
Where Moore, Fair, Bullman, Yerkes, Ammons, fell,
   Thatcher, Smith, and Murphy—names that live not
On gilded historic page, but dwell
   In the hearts of those who stood upon this spot.

At Spottsylvania, where Akerman,
   Lynch, Lindsay, Bisbing, and Sterner went down;
At Cold Harbor, where nature's nobleman
   Gallant Edwin Schall received his golden crown;
Where Mills, Upright, Fizone, and Dunkel died.
   At Petersburg where Cornog and Lenhard,
Fillman, and Davis, too, and Dignan vied
   With Fate to perish before the fierce petard;
At all the battles from Washington down
   To Vicksburg and around again to the sea,
The Fifty-first has won its victor crown
   And shared the glory of a land made free.

Bright are her laurels and great her glory,
　Sacred the pages which record her fame,
Long may they survive to tell their story,
　So free from any taint of vice or shame.

Till round and full their course was run and done,
　As with the Ninth Corps and the mighty hosts
Of the band of freemen who fought and won
　The victory—all their soldiers at their posts—
Petersburg and Richmond yielded their flag—
　And as we all sang praises to the Lord,
Up to the Northern vale and mountain crag,
　Went forth the shout "the Union is restored."

The regiment, with its banners battle-scarred,
　Its tattered flags and trophies stained with gore,
Its men starved, wounded, legless, armless, marred,
　Returned—the wrecks and remnants of the war.—
To lay aside the sword and bayonet,
　To seal the roster as a sacred tome,
And bidding the war sun forever set,
　Fall into the arms of the loved ones home.

But where are they, the fallen ones? the brave
　And noble men who died on hostile field,
Or pined away in prison walls to save
　Our nation's life, or were compelled to yield
Their souls to Heaven with no one near to hear
　Their prayers as they fell to sodden on the sod.
Where are they? Borne on that Seraphic bier,
　Which bears, unquestioned, heroic men to God.

You who have heard brave Reno's ringing voice,
.Who have followed Burnside in the fight,
Have trained with steady Hartranft, whose choice
    And pride you were, as on the left or right,
Or far away from him and us you fought ;
    You, the survivors of this noble band ;
We speak your praise with awe-inspiring thought,
    And pray Heaven to bless you and our native land.

On motion, a vote of thanks was tendered to Captain
J. Merrill Linn, of Lewisburg, Pennsylvania, for his oration, and Hon. George N. Corson, of Norristown, Pennsylvania, for his poem.   Also a vote of thanks to Major
Lane S. Hart, of Harrisburg, for his kind and liberal
offer to print, without cost, in pamphlet form, the proceedings of "The Society of the Fifty-first Regiment,
Pennsylvania Veteran Volunteers," at their first annual
reunion ; to Zook Post, No. 11, for the use of their room ;
to the Humane Fire Engine Company No 1, for the use
of their flags, and to the citizens of Norristown for their
liberal aid.

WILLIAM J. BOLTON,

President.

EDWARD SCHALL,
        Secretary.

COMRADES PRESENT.

Major General John F. Hartranft, . . Philadelphia, Pa.

Major General William J. Bolton, . . Norristown, Pa.

Major Joseph K. Bolton, ... Harrisburg, Pa,

Adjutant Jacob H. Santo, ... Harrisburg, Pa.

Sergeant Major Levi W. Shingle, No.

   255 12th street, ... Philadelphia, Pa.

Commissary Sergeant Levi Bolton, . . Norristown, Pa.

Company " A."

Captain John H. Coulston, . . Wilmington, Del.

First Lieut. Benj. P. Thompson, Harrisburg, Pa.

Second Lieut. Edward L. Evans, Norristown, Pa.

First Sergt. Osman Ortlip, . . . Upper Merion, Pa.

Sergeant Isaac E. Fillmau, . . Norristown, Pa.

Sergeant Washington Smith, . . Royer's Ford, Pa.

Corporal Jesse Herbster, . . . Norristown, Pa.

  " George S. Buzzard, . . Colman, Pa.

  " Hiram C. Lysinger, . Schuylkill, Pa.

  " Amandus Garges, . . Norristown, Pa.

  " John S. Jones, ... Norristown, Pa.

  " Daniel Lare, ... Norristown, Pa.

Private, Baker, George B., . . Conshohocken, Pa.

  " Bolton, James, ... Norristown, Pa.

  " Clair, John, ... Norristown, Pa.

  " Doud, Benjamin F., . Norristown, Pa.

  " Divers, Joseph T., . . Reading, Pa.

  " Dehaven, Isaac, . . . Norristown, Pa.

  " Freas, Samuel H., . . Norristown, Pa.

Private, Gilbert, Theodore, . . Philadelphia, Pa.

"   Goodwin, Jonathan, . . Norristown, Pa.

"   Hallman, Edward, . . Plymouth Meeting, Pa.

"   Heuniss, John, ... Plymouth Meeting, Pa.

"   Hayberry, Charles, . . Plymouth Meeting, Pa.

"   Irwin, Isaac, M. D., . Norristown, Pa.

"   Kellichner, Edwin, . . Conshohocken, Pa.

"   Lare, Albanus, ... Hickorytown, Pa.

"   McCombs, Samuel, . . Norristown, Pa.

"   McKane, William, . . Manayunk, Pa.

"   Parvin, Ephraim, . . Conshohocken, Pa,

"   Toy, Charles, ... Montgomeryville, Pa.

"   Winters, Enos, ... Norristown, Pa.

"   Welsh, John, ... Norristown, Pa.

"   Weber, Jonathan, . . . Norristown, Pa.

"   Widger, George, . . . Norristown, Pa.

"   Widger, Andrew, . . . Philadelphia, Pa.

Company "B."

First Lieut. John Gentner, . . . Easton, Pa.

Corporal Matthew Delaney, . . Easton, Pa.

Private Conrad Schwoerer, No.

    6, Market street, ... Philadelphia, Pa.

Company " C."

Captain William F. Thomas, . . Manayunk, Pa.

First Lieut. George H. Smith, . Harrisburg, Pa.

Sergt. Peter Undercoffler, . . . Collegeville, Pa.

"   William R. Gilbert, . . Norristown, Pa.

Corporal J. Calvin Umstead, . . Royers Ford, Pa.

Corporal Andrew J. Read, . . Pittsburgh, Pa.

" Hugh M. Lynch, . . . Phœnixville, Pa.

" Benjamin R. Sill, . . . Norristown, Pa.

" Hugh McClain, . . Norristown, Pa.

Private, Cook, John J., . . . Philadelphia, Pa.

" Detwiler, Joseph, . . . Roxborough, Pa.

" Fizone, Jacob, . . . Norristown, Pa.

" Fox, William H. R., . Norristown, Pa.

" Fox, Charles R., . . . Norristown, Pa.

" Fillman, Oliver A., . . Norristown, Pa.

" Gunn, William, . . . Phœnixville, Pa.

" Johnson, John, ... Phœnixville, Pa.

" McDade, Patrick, . . . Norristown, Pa.

" Pickup, George, No. 512

    E. Norris street, . . Philadelphia, Pa.

" Peters, Michael, . . . Norristown, Pa.

" Rogan, Patrick, . . . Swedesburg, Pa.

" Springer, John M., . . Norristown, Pa.

" Stout, George, . . . Phœnixville, Pa.

" Sullivan, Patrick, . . . Norristown, Pa.

" Temperly, Thomas, . . Phœnixville, Pa.

" White, Charles, ... Norristown, Pa.

" Wood, Henry P., . . Norristown, Pa.

" Yerger, Mark L., . . . Philadelphia, Pa.

" Undercoffler, Henry, . Collegeville, Pa.

Company " D."

Captain Edward Schall, ... Norristown, Pa.

Captain William W. Owens, . . Norristown, Pa.

First Lieut. John Gilligan, . . Norristown, Pa.

Second Lieut. Jonathan Swallow, Norristown, Pa.

Sergeant William D. Jenkins, . . Norristown, Pa.

     "   John McNulty, . . . Conshohocken, Pa.

     "   Walter M. Thompson, . Phœnixville, Pa.

     "   Penrose W. Clair, . . . Blue Bell, Pa.

Corporal John L. McCoy, . . Norristown, Pa.

     "   Andrew Fair, ... Norristown, Pa.

     "   Nicholas Murphy, . . . Norristown, Pa.

     "   Albert List, ... Lewisburg, Pa.

     "   ·John Sutch, ... Roxborough, Pa.

Private, Beswick, Charles, . . . Norristown, Pa.

     "   Cornog, Addison, . . . Norristown, Pa.

     "   Dunbar, Thomas, . . . Norristown, Pa.

     "   Diamond, Patrick, . . Norristown, Pa.

     "   Earl, John, ... Conshohocken, Pa.

     "   Fizone, Mordecai, . . Norristown, Pa.

     "   Fleck, John R., . . . Norristown, Pa.

     "   Geyer, John R., . . . Norristown, Pa.

     "   Lukens, Ellwood, . . . Norristown, Pa.

     "   Lysinger, Charles, . . Norristown, Pa.

     "   Montgomery, Thomas J., Schuylkill Falls, Pa.

     "   McDade, William, . . Norristown, Pa.

     "   McDade, Samuel, . . . Norristown, Pa.

     "   McManamy, William, . Norristown, Pa.

     "   Standenmayer, Jacob,
           care C. and P. R. R., Pittsburgh, Pa.

     "   Sutch, Henry, ... Collegeville, Pa.

     "   Vanfossen, Hiram, . . Norristown, Pa.

     "   Widger, Charles, . . . Norristown, Pa.

     "   Yost, Daniel B., . . . Norristown, Pa.

Company " E."

Second Lieut. Martin L. Schock, New Berlin, Pa.
Sergt. E. G. Maize, No. 818 Chest-
      nut street, ... Philadelphia, Pa.
Musician Joseph A. Logan, . . Milton, Pa.

Company " F."

Captain Jacob P. Brooke, . . Lewisburg, Pa.
Second Lieut. Henry Jacobs, . Norristown, Pa.
First Sergt. William B. Hart, . Harrisburg, Pa.
Sergt. Jacob W. Reed, ... Lansdale, Pa.
Corporal Silas Kulp, ... Green Lane, Pa.
    "   Thomas B. Yerger, . . Norristown, Pa.
    "   Henry C. Hughes, . . Norristown, Pa.
Musician William C. Hansell, . Camden, N. J.
    "   Lyle Franklin, ... Bridgeport, Pa.
Private, Baird, James S. . . . Norristown, Pa.
    "   Daub, George W., . . Norristown, Pa.
    "   Daub, Samuel G., . . . Norristown, Pa.
    "   Earl, Alexander D., . . Philadelphia, Pa.
    "   Freas, Daniel, ... Conshohocken, Pa.
    "   Hansell, George Y., . . Washington, D. C.
    "   Holmes, George W., . Norristown, Pa.
    "   Johns, Edwin M., . . . Norristown, Pa.
    "   Kremer, Frederick, . . Norristown, Pa.
    "   Lewis, William H., . . Norristown, Pa.
    "   McClennan, Samuel, . Norristown, Pa.
    "   McCarter, Samuel, . . Norristown, Pa.
    "   McFadden, Francis, . . Norristown, Pa.

Private, Reed, Edwin M., No.
     420 North Second st., Philadelphia, Pa.
  " Taylor, Samuel, . . . Norristown, Pa.
  " Thompson, Charles, . . Norristown, Pa.
  " Workeizer, William, . . Norristown, Pa.

Company " G."

Captain William H. Blair, . . . Bellefonte, Pa.

Company " H."

Captain J. Merrill Linn, ... Lewisburg, Pa.
First Lieut. William F. Campbell, Allenwood, Pa.
Sergt. Daniel M. Wetzel, . . Grand Rapids, Mich.
Private Anthony Weisenbach, . Norristown, Pa.

Company " I."

Captain George R. Pechin, . . . Norristown, Pa.
First Lieut. George Schall, . . Norristown, Pa.
  " Lewis Patterson, . . Swedeland, Pa.
First Sergt. George Carney, . . Norristown, Pa.
Sergeant William Pope, ... Upper Merion.
  " James Cameron, . . . Upper Merion.
  " Andrew S. Leedom, . . Conshohocken, Pa.
Corporal John M. Engle, . . . West Conshohocken.
  " James Y. Shainline, . . Norristown, Pa.
Musician James Chase, ... Norristown, Pa.
Private, Cornog, Thomas, . . . Upper Merion, Pa.
  " Detterline, Joseph, . . Norristown, Pa.
  " Edwards, Samuel, . . . ————————, Pa.
  " Glisson, George W., . . Norristown, Pa.
  " Powers, Charles, . . . Norristown, Pa.
  " Pluck, Jacob, ... Norristown, Pa.

Company "K."

Private, Crites, William H., . . Huntingdon, Pa.
"   Dittler, John C., . . . Easton, Pa.

CPSIA information can be obtained
at www.ICGtesting.com
Printed in the USA
BVHW04*1018190918
527934BV00014B/1046/P